The Parent's Guide

to

College Admissions

Success

The Parent's Guide

to

College Admissions

Success

Key Strategies from an Admissions Expert

By: Shereem Herndon-Brown, MA

This book is dedicated to all of my students—past, present and future. You inspire me every day.

TABLE OF CONTENTS

MEET THE AUTHOR

Shereem Herndon-Brown started Herndon-Brown Consulting in 2006, which eventually became Strategic Admissions Advice in 2009. Keying in on his experiences as a former college admissions officer at Georgetown University and school counselor at Riverdale Country School and Westtown School, the transition to an independent college coach was a natural progression. He has worked with students from all over the world, having recently traveled to China. He has worked with the children of billionaires, spoken at national conferences, mentored students in underprivileged communities and taught at the Independent Educational Consultants Association Summer Training Institute.

As a dynamic leader, educational strategist, and emerging author and speaker, his experiences in the field are unparalleled. As an educator for nearly twenty years and an entrepreneur for almost a decade, he has counseled many students and families through the often-frustrating admissions maze that is private schools and colleges.

Inspiring and instructional, Shereem connects with anyone who needs an educational plan. His students have attended schools such as Dartmouth, Duke, Emory, Harvard, Stanford, Syracuse, University of Georgia, University of Miami, University of Michigan, University of Pennsylvania, University of Virginia,

University of Texas (Austin), Vanderbilt, Yale, as well as many others.

Having worked on both sides of the desk in admissions, Shereem has a perspective that few other counselors have. He aims to assist students and families who do not readily know about this process or have extensive knowledge of the world of private school and college education. He clearly has his finger on the pulse of what is most important to families, and is consistently strategic in his approach to helping students to have school choices.

He is a graduate of Wesleyan University, with a Bachelor of Arts degree in English and a Masters of Arts degree from the Breadloaf School of English at Middlebury College. In 2005, he was selected by the National Association of Independent Schools as an E.E. Ford Fellow for Aspiring Heads of School. Additionally, he has served on the Board of Trustees at La Cima Elementary Charter School in his native Brooklyn, New York. He is also Member of the Independent Educational Consulting Association (IECA), Southern Association of College Admissions Counseling (SACAC), and the National Association of College Admissions Counseling (NACAC). He has been quoted in the *New York Times*, *Washington Post* and *Chicago Tribune*, and written for both *Suwanee Magazine* and *Uptown Magazine*.

Shereem enjoys reading, exercising, traveling and playing with his wife and four children. He is an active member of his church, an avid sports fan, and a distinguished member of Omega Psi Phi Fraternity Incorporated. *"*

Every student I have ever worked with has had college choices."

A Word on Success

I have been involved in college counseling and college admissions for twenty years, and I can tell you right now there is no magic pill. There is no secret strategy to getting anyone into Harvard, Yale, Princeton or Stanford. What there is, however, is preparation and not-so-secret strategies that will lead to college admissions success. It also depends on how you define success.

I define success by the availability of choices—college choices. When young people have guidance about their college and career options, they tend to make better choices. In order to have three choices, they need to think big. They need to think about the game plans for their lives and about life strategies that will lead to success.

Being strategic means being organized, intentional, and assertive. Strategizing to achieve goals is necessary to prepare for success. Even if your child is someone who thinks that successful people— people with a plethora of choices—are just lucky, remember the words of the philosopher Seneca: *"Luck is when preparation meets opportunity."*

To learn more about Strategic Admissions Advice, visit us at strategicadmissionsadvice.com

Chapter 1

STRATEGIC PLANNING: PARENT

"You cannot 'hope' that your child gets into the college of his or her dreams. You must prepare."

STRATEGIC PLANNING: PARENT

My question to parents who want to support their children in the college application process is, "How do you plan to win?"

Hope is Not a Plan

You cannot "hope" your child gets into the college of his or her dreams. You must prepare.

Take a moment to think about why you picked up this book. You may be overseeing your oldest child's departure to college or looking into different tactics to help your youngest child in the application process. This book aims to help you every step of the way.

"The most important thing parents need to keep in mind is that college, and the process of getting in, should be driven by the student."

It is likely that you have been preparing for this moment in your child's educational life since he or she was born. You are determined. You have worked hard and made sacrifices. You will do anything and everything you can to help your child lead a successful life. You believe that success in life starts with a stellar education. Now you are at a critical point, and it is time to consider which colleges may be right for your child.

The college admissions process, and college itself, is about the applicant taking ownership. This is your child's life, education, and decision. If you are uncomfortable giving your child the reins right now, when will you be

ready to do so? After college? During grad school? When they're choosing a spouse? Once upon a time, being eighteen meant a sense of autonomy, and as a culture, we have gotten away from that. The most important thing parents need to keep in mind is that college, and the process of getting in, should be driven by the student.

As a parent, it is your job to help your child as much as possible, but once the applications are out and decisions are made, the choice needs to rest with your child. Hopefully, as you and your child navigate the process together, you both will gain a mutual trust that the best decisions are being made.

Here's the Plan:
Assessment + Strategy = College Choices

Did you pick up this book because you want to know how to get your child into an Ivy League school? While a great goal, I want to make clear that my role as an independent counselor is not to guarantee your child's admission into any particular school. My services are to assess what your child's strengths and interests are, suggest schools that may help your child grow as a student and person, and strategize authentic ways to present themselves to a college and execute their application. Independent counselors who tell you they will ensure your child's admittance into a certain school are lying to themselves, and even more importantly, to you. Year-by-year and step-by-step, I will provide you with details on making the most of your time and planning ahead.

Prepare for Competition

"The coveted spots at the top schools are for those who will benefit the college in some way."

Throughout my years in this profession, lack of preparation is the number one reason why I have seen students fail. What's the solution? PREPARATION!!! My team and I will push your child to be the best they can be. We will ask tough questions, and we expect real answers. If your child follows our suggestions, the process will not be as daunting during the late summer/early fall of senior year.

As parents, by arming yourselves with simple information as early as possible in your child's high school career, you are getting a head start and a leg up. But do not confuse preparation and diligence with making a bigger deal out of this than you should. You have worked hard to educate your child and to give them everything you ever had, and more. This same impulse to have them enjoy the best possible options will also be at work as they explore colleges, but it will serve them best if you remain calm and supportive throughout the process.

The college application process is competitive. There are more incredibly talented students in the country than there are seats at the most selective schools. These schools are the *best* because they often have the best resources: the most sought-after faculty, the most distinguished alumni, and the most renowned programs.

The coveted spots at the top schools are for those who will benefit the college in some way. Schools want students with academic prowess, athletes, legacies (children of alumni), development cases (children of potential donors), and under-represented minorities. Let's face it: nothing is free. If your child wants to absorb the information and experience that a college can give, your child will need to give something back. In many ways, colleges are big business.

Yes, colleges hire smart people to teach courses, and they offer a relatively safe haven for students aged eighteen through twenty-three. Yes, they are places for young adults to grow, nurture, and cultivate their professional aspirations. But beware: colleges want to win, too. They want smart students who will be potential leaders in a variety of industries. They want these same students, now alumni, to wave the flag of their institution, sport their sweatshirt, or place decals on their car—all of which will ultimately raise the school's profile and increase its popularity.

Now that you're sufficiently nervous, I will flip and say that colleges and their administrators are not soulless, greedy, manipulative places and people. Colleges are educational environments with dedicated educators who want young people to excel. However, they do have operating costs and bills. Without the exorbitant tuition they charge and the capital campaigns to bring in even more dollars, they would not have the ability to do what they do so well, and in turn, attract new students and families. The bottom line is that the relationship with a college is reciprocal: the college needs your child just as much as your child needs the college.

The Strategic Admissions Road Map

Our preparation process for parents is thorough and falls into two parts. (Be sure to grab your free Strategic Admissions Road Map at: strategicadmissionsadvice.com/bookstore) **First, work to expose your child to the idea of college before high school**. Whether they watch college football on Saturdays on ESPNU, or you accompany them on a visit to the school that you or a family member attended, they need to know that college exists and that attending college is an attainable goal for them. Explain to them that the goal of college is to expand their minds and introduce them to people and ideas that will help them personally and professionally. Delve into the importance of networking in college —the relationships built during four years on a campus can greatly impact their professional path in the years to come.

Capture your student's attention by relating college to the prospect of higher education and life opportunity. Explain to them that if they do not go to college, the likelihood they will have the career trajectory of others who do go to college is minimal. In fact, a *New York Times* article from 2013 examined a law firm that commits to only hiring graduates from four-year colleges, even for menial "runner" type jobs. Their reasoning is people who go to college are more motivated as well as goal- and career-oriented than those who do not. Another reason is the poor job market and intense competition for available jobs. As one recruiter in the article put it, "When eight hundred applicants apply for a job, there has to be a way to weed some of them out. Having a bachelor's degree is one way to avoid that type of preliminary cut."

An important conversation to have with your child is one about the value of a college experience. Having a college degree does not guarantee wealth. Going to college puts your child in an environment with other young people who are similarly motivated to creating life options and open to stimulating their own minds. I know several people who did not go to college and who are happy and/or wealthy. I know even more people who honestly believe that college is a waste of time and money. My question to these unique people is—where do they want their child to be between the ages of eighteen and twenty-five? Do they want them to get "a job"? Enlist in the military? Do they have the resources to train them in their family business and/or give them startup costs for their own business? If they do—great. If that works for a lifetime, even better! Yet, most of the people we admire in life for their peace of mind, health, and wealth educated themselves somehow; they spent formidable years studying something to give them the fulfillment they are enjoying now. If it did not happen on a college campus or in a classroom, trust they had the luxury of reading, brainstorming, or trying myriad ways to make things work. They either had institutional or rigorous practical education, and they are who they are because of this learning.

"For all of the commotion that is made about Harvard, Princeton and Yale, it is neither fair to your child nor to your sanity to predetermine that your child's fate in life hinges on their admittance to those schools."

My second step in the preparation process is the practical side: *determine when your child should start getting serious about academics.* To actually be a strong candidate for the fifty (or so) most prestigious colleges in the United States, the preparation process actually begins in the eighth grade. Yes, when your child chooses classes for the eighth grade, the assigned track for science, math and foreign language may eventually impact what classes are taken as a ninth grader and, in turn, that may affect the rigor of your child's entire high school transcript. Certain colleges, particularly Ivy League schools and those similar to them, may expect that an applicant have taken calculus as a senior. That means your child will need to take geometry as a freshman, algebra 2/trigonometry as a sophomore, pre-calculus as a junior, and calculus as a senior. This is a traditional formula that may or may not be applicable at your high school, but is a tried and true expectation of some of the most prestigious schools in the country.

At the same time, I do not suggest becoming too invested in a particular school or "league" of schools—especially if your child only knows their names by reputation. There are plenty of great colleges that do not follow the traditional formula. As a country, we have become obsessed with what college can and should do for our future generations. For all of the commotion that is made about Harvard, Princeton and Yale, it is neither fair to your child nor to your sanity to predetermine that your child's fate in life hinges on admittance to those schools. I have parents who tell me their seventh grader will be their "Ivy League" child, but they do not realize the intense pressure they unintentionally apply to the child and to themselves. Instead, take a look at the thirty-five hundred great schools and programs across the country and find one that will suit your child's individual academic and social needs.

Also, consider your child's needs in high school from the perspective of a teenager. As Americans, we value our high school experiences very much. Adults tend to have either fond memories of high school or troubling ones; but regardless, most of us admit that our unique experiences shaped us tremendously. Although we all undergo change throughout the years, high school is memorable and pivotal in our development. This will be the same for your child. Do you want your child to spend all of their time studying? Or, do you want them to find a happy balance between fun, teenage stuff and hard work?

Chapter 2

STRATEGIC PLANNING: STUDENT

"Colleges are expecting your child to have the best grades possible."

STRATEGIC PLANNING: STUDENT

Parents, try reading this section with your kid. Yes, I know he or she may roll their eyes at the thought of discussing college, but this is the one part that I hope students grasp. It's written to you, but it's for them.

High school matters. No matter what anyone tells you or your child —"you have plenty of time," "have fun, relax; you're a teenager"—please know that what is done in high school will influence your child's life. That is not to sound morbid or proclaim doom and gloom: it is simply a wake-up call.

Most grown-ups will admit, "If I knew then what I know now...." Too many of us bemoan decisions we made in high school and wish we had taken a different path. That is not to say that there is one path that is right and the others are wrong, but some pitfalls may have been and can be avoided by being proactive in the present.

Having a life of purpose and direction is a wonderful thing. No, I am not telling you that your child needs to decide what "job" they will have forever; I am only encouraging you to help them think about their future and choose to create choices.

"Having good grades does not make someone a good person, but it does provide them the flexibility of having choices once school is over."

To prepare your child to get into college, here is what they need to know and act on:

1. **Grades Matter**
2. **Standardized Test Scores Matter**
3. **How Time is Spent Matters**
4. **Being Artistic Matters**
5. **Being an Athlete Matters**
6. **Being Innovative or Entrepreneurial Matters**
7. **Use of Social Media Matters**
8. **Majors Matter**

(Don't miss out on this infographic: strategicadmissionsadvice.com/bookstore)

Grades Matter

Throughout life, people are told to get good grades. Most often, people who get good grades get recognition and awards. Good grades often equal respect from peers and teachers. It means a person can listen, read, and is informed. We feel proud when our children get good grades, and they feel proud of themselves. Most importantly, however, colleges expect the best grades possible.

The process of studying hard and well—of acquiring and exercising strong study skills—will serve your children well in college and beyond. They will know how to prepare; they know they have to sit and learn and be prepared to share what they know with someone else. In practicing a career as a doctor, a salesperson, a musician, or a lawyer, they will have to do these same things. Your children must know their "stuff" and have the confidence and know-how to shine when called upon.

Having good grades provides them the flexibility of having choices once high school is over. Very few colleges will admit students who are consistently struggling in school, especially during their junior and senior years. Colleges want students who are ready to go to class and contribute—students who will graduate and use their school as a catapult into whatever their career may be. If you are reading this, and your child is not yet applying to colleges and his or her grades could be better, please stress that underperforming closes doors and reduces options. Good performance creates opportunity and choices.

Standardized Test Scores Matter

I am not a good standardized test taker: never have been and I do not expect I ever will be. Despite the ongoing debates about whether standardized testing is good and what purpose it serves, it is unlikely standardized testing can be avoided.

So what can be done? Since your child will have to take them, start understanding how they work. Preparation is key with standardized testing, as with anything in life. There are many free—yes, free—resources to help you and your child understand these tests better and create an advantage in taking them. Professional test preparation is also available. Now, that does not mean that SAT or ACT test prep needs to begin in kindergarten. But it can start as early as seventh grade. If your child has not started and is in the ninth or tenth grade, why not start today? Go to Khanacademy.org or Collegeboard.org or ACT.org and get familiar with the types of test questions. There are even phone apps available to download to assist with preparation (SAT question of the day). I will delve further into test preparation in Chapter 5.

So, if high school matters, and to excel in high school your child's scores matter, you need to take standardized tests seriously. If you or your child is adamant that testing and test prep culture is ridiculous and want no part of it, I understand; just know that, in the long run, your child's options will be more limited. Most colleges want test scores. Most high schools require end-of-year standardized tests. Many colleges have standardized placement exams for their courses. Standardized tests are a part of education, right or wrong, so please do play the game to win. Start preparing now.

If your child is like me and does not test well, know that there are still many schools options out there. Some schools are score optional, meaning you do not have to submit test scores, and hence, never have to take the test. Bates College, and American and Wake Forest Universities are just three such schools, so do not fret that college is not for your child if testing is not his or her forte. Different schools have different entrance test policies and different expectations. Therefore, high school transcripts, which can be made impressive throughout four years of high school, can speak loudly about academic abilities in the absence of standardized test scores. Although standardized test scores are part of the picture, how a student performs day in and day out speaks volumes about not just ability, but also work ethic and attitude. The combination of solid grades and respectable test scores makes a student a convincingly desirable candidate. For the list of colleges and universities that are test-optional or test-flexible, visit the National Center for Fair and Open Testing's website at www.fairtest.org.

How Time is Spent Matters

What does your child like to do outside of school? Play sports? Create in the art studio? Volunteer with a church, synagogue or a local organization? Participate in clubs and other activities that school offers (band, theater, Model UN, robotics)?

Colleges are communities. Whether they are comprised of forty thousand people, like a huge state school, or fifteen hundred students, like a small college, they consist of young people who will be living and learning together for a set amount of time. College admissions offices want graduating high school seniors to contribute to their college communities. Colleges use high school activities to indicate potential college activities.

A student who goes to school and goes home will not be attractive to a college. Even with good grades, a one-dimensional student— meaning one who only does homework—has little appeal. Having interests beyond the classroom helps a student become a well-rounded person, which is attractive to colleges.

If you ask, "What about the football player who is one-dimensional? All he does is play football!" —then it is not true. He does two things: he has to go to class and remain eligible for the football team, which makes him a student-athlete. He may also have to participate in fundraisers for the team or mentor younger players in the community who aspire to play football for the high school. Yes, I know athletes are often celebrated ad nauseam in our culture and it seems unfair, but it is not accurate to call them one-dimensional. Even for the best athletes, if they're not doing what they're supposed to do in the classroom, they will not be able to play.

Your children should set about becoming multi-dimensional once in high school:

- **Explore options.** What do their schools offer? What can they do in their communities? Whether your students are athletes, artists or budding scientists, have them do some research. Your children need to put themselves out there and meet people who have similar interests. Your children will learn from them and they will learn from your children.

- **Your students need to be curious and try new activities.** One of the things I wish I had explored in high school and college is theater. But I saw it as anti-athlete, and I viewed myself as strictly a student, an athlete, a newspaper writer, and a community leader. Now, I honestly wish I had tried the stage because it would have allowed me to develop useful skills such as commanding the attention of an

- audience with speech. So many of us fear what we do not know. Maybe your child's gifts are artistic—singing, theater, and so on—and it would benefit them to become just a little uncomfortable and explore these areas, because guess what? Actors are celebrated in our culture and most of us love TV and movies.

   Who knows, maybe your child will find his or her calling and be a "thespian" (great SAT word!).

- **Work.** Simply put, being self-sufficient is a great attribute for a student to possess. Colleges are very impressed with students who have chosen to work. Taking life seriously and earning their way shows schools that they do not want everything handed to them. Moreover, balancing work with good grades and scores shows an ability to manage time well, a skill that is essential to succeeding in college.

- **Your students should volunteer where they want to make a difference.** They should never, ever, ever, do community service to look good. While colleges will not know how or why they did some kind of service, they themselves will know, and the organizer or leader will know, and they will not want them there for very long. They should always volunteer in order to do work that matters to them. If they love animals, work at a pet rescue.

If they like children, volunteer with a local elementary school or after-school program. If they value spiritual health and community, serve at a church, temple or mosque. Volunteering will be impressive to colleges, but more than anything, it will make them feel good about contributing to the world.

Being Artistic Matters

Most people associate college with education, sports, parties and careers. Although much of that is true, college can also be about enriching life artistically. There are many art schools and conservatories of dance and music that need students interested who are in the arts. They were built to accommodate the artist—the painter, the dancer, the graphic designer, and so on. Some even have web design majors. All of these artistic educational hubs have plenty of interested and capable students enrolled each year, and they get these qualified students from high schools where portfolios and talents are developed.

Many adults freeze with fear when someone talks about being an artist in college and beyond. Their hesitation is usually based on the assumption that the artist, no matter their medium, will be poor and unable to earn a living. That is not necessarily true—there are many employed actors, singers, and visual artists who have had tertiary education—and honing this craft in college can be a worthwhile investment in the future.

Being an Athlete Matters

It is not only football and basketball players who matter. Wrestlers, fencers, cheerleaders and swimmers are all great sports for your child to participate in while in high school. Although many of these sports are not recruitable for college, they signal to colleges that these students possess the discipline needed to work with a team to achieve a goal—a skill integral to success in college and beyond.

Colleges like to see commitment to a sport or activity for an extended period of time. Students who rise from the freshman team to the junior varsity and then to varsity have committed ample time to their sport of choice. That twelve-to-fifteen hour-per-week commitment will not be overlooked by a college admissions office.

If your student has potential to be a recruited athlete, consider which school matches the student's skill level. Not everyone can play basketball at a Southeastern Conference school, so your child might consider a smaller school, possibly outside of your immediate geographic area. It may be a good college experience both academically and athletically.

Regardless, it is important for both parent and athlete to know the National Collegiate Athletic Association (NCAA) rules and regulations for recruitment and eligibility. Many student-athletes with hopes and dreams for a Division I career initially overlook the value of Division III programs, where there is often better balance between athletics and academics. There are very strict rules that have to be adhered to when beginning the sophomore year of school.

High schools and colleges rally around athletes because their performance often instills tremendous school pride. Colleges want to know these students have been part of lifting the school's spirit in some capacity and that they may do the same for their school. Additionally, remember that colleges are businesses; they need fans—people to play in intramural teams and happy parents of students to donate to them. Being recruitable to a college sports team makes an attractive applicant.

Being Innovative or Entrepreneurial Matters

Startup companies are now ubiquitous. The paradigm of the workforce has changed, and younger people firmly believe they have the next big idea and want to run their own company. This entrepreneurial spirit is an incredible attribute for students applying to college for two reasons: colleges love something novel and distinguishable. If, for instance, the student has a model business—

in reality or an idea—one in which will do the world, community, or country some greater good, that student is already ahead of the competition in terms of application appearance. When all applicants are reduced to between four and seven sheets of paper, the memorable ones are those who are different. Most seventeen-year-olds are not fully ready to embrace entrepreneurial endeavors, so the ones who have will stand out.

I caution you to advise your children not to create a business website that serves solely to "impress" a school; it will not. However, if your child has a product or a service, or the blueprint of an idea that he or she can articulate well, please have them share it via some appropriate means. Colleges like young people who are active thinkers and who want to change the world. And, if the idea is successful, the school will benefit from free publicity!

Use of Social Media Matters

The world has welcomed social media with open arms as a wonderful form of communication and information broadcast tool. It is rare to find someone today who is not on Facebook, Twitter, Instagram, Pinterest, Vine or Snapchat—to name a few. It is essential for your children, with much of their lives still in front of them, to remember that information shared on social media is often public or can quickly be made public. What is shared and how it is shared may be interpreted by people who were not the intended audience.

The way a student is represented in the digital world might be the first and lasting (maybe even last!) impression someone has. They say think twice before speaking; tell your child to think thrice before posting on social media. Pose this question to your son or daughter: "If you did not know yourself and read that post you just made, what would it make you think about the person sharing it?" All social media posts and conversations should be ones that would not disqualify him or her from a college admissions opportunity if the admissions team were to read them.

Students should be especially careful to never cyber-bully others. Not only is this unkind, it will be hard to make a case that a bully is a student this dream college needs in their upcoming class!

Majors Matter

"Students who use their last two years of high school to outline an educational plan with clear academic goals are more focused and successful during college."

The expectations of a college education are changing. Once upon a time, students and parents alike were content with college being an exploratory time in a young person's life. Students were encouraged to experience a variety of academic disciplines with the hope that one would resonate and lead to the declaration of a major and usher the way to a career. This phenomenon of using college to "find yourself," however, is rapidly evaporating. Every year, a few students call me after a semester or two of college and ask, "What should I do?" These are the same students who were adamant about using college to expose themselves to an array of courses and are now, unfortunately, recognizing that time flies and big life decisions need to be made quickly. While I laud their initial academic curiosity, it pains me to see them scrambling to take the prerequisites that will allow them to declare and complete a major in time for graduation.

Students who use their last two years of high school to outline an educational plan with clear academic goals are more focused and successful during college. Their full immersion into their classes makes their academic experience more enjoyable and eases the transition to a career post-college. For years, I have helped students recognize that college is a short portion of their life experience. It should be taken seriously, and going in with a sense of purpose and a potential major in mind is the ideal.

I am a firm believer that students should take courses and decide on a major that will motivate them to learn. This is not a "one size fits all" situation. Most successful and happy people will tell you that being a learner—someone who keeps an active and growing mind—is what makes them happy. Each day, they should be enriching their minds by, for instance, reading, playing educational computer games, or doing math equations.

So how can a student identify a potential major? There are many personality and career assessment tools available online that can help students gauge fields for which they are most suited. Many students have access to Naviance at their schools, and many independent educational consultants use tests like *Major Match* or *YouScience.* At Strategic Admissions Advice, we too use an online survey that analyzes data and generates a report based on a student's strengths and interests; suggestions for majors and careers are based on stable personality traits rather than ever-changing interests and abilities. We believe that this tool provides useful information about what a student should pursue with regard to courses, majors and careers.

As an admissions officer, I was always impressed with high school students who knew what they wanted to do in college. Their application became powerful. Now, as an independent education consultant, I actively discourage my students from choosing "undecided" when given the option to indicate an area of academic interest on their applications. The operative word here is "interest"; your child should select something that is of genuine "interest" to him or her. Selecting "undecided" is an easy way to lead colleges to assume that your child lacks focus, and makes his or her application look unremarkable. Colleges want students who are engaged and hungry to learn. If your child is such a student, advise him or her not to be "undecided"—be "interested."

"By indicating an academic interest, high school applicants are simply taking a bit of control over the admissions process and defining themselves in the way that they want to be seen."

Ask any college what are they looking for in an applicant, and they usually reply saying that they are looking for students to diversify a class. They need different kids from varied backgrounds, with wide-ranging interests and abilities. Just as they may need a new quarterback and/or bassoonist, they also need an aspiring environmentalist and/or architect. The only way for a college to determine who will add this intellectual value is by gleaning what applicants express for a likely major, and what they write about in an essay.

Please do not think that once students indicate a potential major or academic interest when applying to a school, they are bound forever. Most colleges give students until the end of their sophomore year to declare a major.

Of course, not all students are the same, and some—even after doing personality tests—may still have no clue about which courses to take, which major to declare, or which career to pursue. That's more than okay. Even for students who are truly undecided, they should still seek to understand their strengths and interests, as well as their options.

Now, why should they do this? With proper guidance, these students will begin to identify schools that make better matches for them than others. Colleges and college admission strategies are not "one size fits all," but it never hurts to have concrete suggestions on how to maximize their college academic experience. It passes quickly.

Chapter 3

THE FOUR BIG QUESTIONS

"Four years go quickly, but they can seem to drag on forever if your child is in a place where he or she is genuinely unhappy."

THE FOUR BIG QUESTIONS

"Parents usually ask me The Four Big Questions because their children ask them those same ones."

When parents of high school students find out what I do, there are usually four questions they want answered when it comes to their child's college education:

1. What Should I Do?
2. Where Should My Child Go?
3. How Does My Child Get In?
4. How Do We Pay for It?

That's it! Every question I have ever answered fits into these four categories. Sure, there may sub-categories for each, but these are parents' most popular queries.

Parents usually ask me The Four Big Questions because their children ask them those same ones. So, how can I best answer these questions? I start by sharing information, which leads to parents and applicants diving into preparation. Once students and families are armed with information about which schools are out there and which programs are great matches for the applicant, they are fired up about how they (with our counsel) can come out on the winning end of the college assessment, search, and application processes.

What Should I Do?

Plan strategically so you can guide your child as needed.

I have already explained what you need to do to support your child. Additionally, in Chapter 3, I relayed what your child should do in high school in order to become a successful college applicant. I will delve into greater detail about what they should be doing in each grade in Chapter 6. Now, with your child, let's consider the remaining three questions.

Where Should My Child Go?

Where no one else will—or, at least, where no one else from your area will go.

Think geographic diversity: colleges are frequently looking to diversify their enrollment based on race, class, gender, socioeconomic status, and yes, geography. There is a resource, "Freshman Class Locator," that I use to show parents and students which states where students in first-year classes come from. Take the University of Michigan, for instance. It is a state school and pulls in a lot of kids from the Midwest. It also pulls in kids from New York and California. So how about a kid from Arkansas or Idaho? Based on strong grades, solid scores, and intriguing activities, should Michigan be interested in this student? Should they want to have a kid from Arkansas on their campus so when this student goes home, this student can tell all of his or her friends about this awesome experience in Ann Arbor? The answer is clear —yes!

Going where others don't dare go is strategic, but it must be balanced with going where the student will hopefully be happy. This is a healthy move. Four years go quickly, but they can seem to drag on forever at a place in which the student is genuinely unhappy. Going to a college that is the wrong fit can mean not making it to graduation (colleges have retention and attrition rates for a reason). When choosing a school, your students should be in tune with a gut feeling that they love their culture on this campus. That is why it is important to talk with alums and current students, and to visit whenever possible. Does your student abhor cliques? A school with an ingrained, active, and uncontrolled Greek life might not be a good fit. This student would be more comfortable in a school that bans frats and sororities, or one where those groups are not allowed to color the culture of the whole school. Does winter make your child depressed? If so, it is important that your child goes to a school where it is sunny year round so that more time is not spent in the health center than in classes. Do big cities like New York make your child feel motivated to study or motivated to party?

Help your child choose a school that will help them achieve their after-college goals. Do they want to open a business on the day they graduate from college? Choose the school that has a great track record of turning out entrepreneurs, or the one that will give them the skills, knowledge, and networks that great entrepreneurs need. By the way, one of the best things about college is the network of connections made with other budding professionals. Does your child want to pursue med school afterwards? Look for schools with supportive medical studies committees and an admirable percentage of med school aspirants who eventually get their dream career. Does your child have no idea what to do after college? Then, they should go to a college whose core or general education requirements won't crowd out time to try classes that are of interest. Above all, keep in mind that one of the surest ways to be able to use college to obtain future goals is to do well there and garner glowing recommendations to follow the student. So simply, students need to choose colleges where they can clearly manage both academic and social lives, have opportunities to grow and contribute to the campus, and get to form meaningful relationships with some professors and peers.

How Does My Child Get In?

By presenting his or her authentic and best self.

This is the applicant's greatest asset in the college application process. Once again, the best way to do this is through the indication of a major.

Be advised, however: by choosing a popular major, your student enters a more competitive pool. Some schools do not admit freshmen based upon their indicated major as an applicant, but many do. It is, therefore, wise for you and your child to educate yourselves on which schools consider this. Know which major is most popular where, and be sure to go after at least some schools where the student's academic interest stands out.

The best version of the student, as a complement to the most unique version, should also have significant and authentic civic engagement. In other words, service—the kind in which a person makes an earnest attempt to make a change in the community.

How Do We Pay For It?

You can't talk about college without talking about money. College is expensive. So, this question often depends on the college's cost of attendance.

Every college uses a figure called Cost of Attendance (COA) to calculate what it will cost a student to attend. This includes tuition, fees, room and board, books, supplies, transportation, and personal expenses. They also use this figure to determine financial aid packages.

Colleges also use something called the Expected Family Contribution (EFC). The EFC is a formula that analyzes a family's income and assets to determine the annual amount a family is obligated to contribute toward college costs. If the student is a dependent of the parent, the EFC includes the parental contribution and the student's contribution. Each family's expected contribution is different because every family has a different financial situation.

Depending on a family's standing, the student might have Eligibility for Aid ('need'). This is the COA minus EFC. Some colleges solely provide financial aid based upon need. Some combine need with 'merit aid'—the latter being based on a student's achievements. If a college's aid package does not meet the student's full need, there is a 'gap' that also has to be covered by you or your child.

The EFC plus the gap expense is the amount the family has to 'pay for college.' Parent and student loans are the most popular methods of covering this expense.

If the EFC and gap amounts are relatively low, students might find that on-campus, part-time, or summer employment can help them pay their way through college. Some students also choose accelerated tracks where possible, such as completing four years' worth of coursework in three years; this method of saving expenses might not be worth it if it places the students under pressure that negatively affects their academic performance.

Some students also apply for external merit scholarships offered by foundations as well as religious and community groups. Some students turn to online fundraising from family and friends and crowd funding. Scholarship search engines and scholarship search apps are ubiquitous. Have your child sign up for updates from a couple of these services. They will need to keep a database of eligible scholarships and start putting together applications in junior year. You and your child can inform people you know to be on the lookout for scholarships, and have your child apply early. Where there is a will, you and your child will create a way!

Chapter 4

THE
COLLEGE APPLICATION

"The good news is that your child can excel at any college and use the time there as a springboard to a successful life."

THE COLLEGE APPLICATION

Applications must be submitted on time and must stand out.

There are five critical pieces to almost every college application:

1. **The Transcript/Grades**

2. **Standardized Test Scores**

3. **Extracurricular Resumes**

4. **Recommendations from school teachers and school guidance counselors**

5. **Essays** *(I say "essays" because many of the top schools ask for a personal essay as well as supplemental essays)*

1. The Transcript

I want to start with the transcript because it is—and always has been—the most important part of the application. Grades are a reflection of how well students have chosen courses, appropriately challenged themselves, and consistently performed at a high level. Now, if you or your students are groaning because their grades are not perfect, do not fret. There are still colleges for these students. It might not be Harvard or Yale, but do not let the past dictate the future. The transcript is not the only element in the application, but it is a heavily weighted piece of information that every college will want.

2. Standardized Test Scores

As you know, there are schools—very good, prestigious schools that do not require SAT or ACT scores. Understanding the requirements of test-optional schools helps alleviate some confusion surrounding standardized testing. Not understanding which tests meet which school's requirements deters many students from even applying.

A bit of a reality check: some people have deduced that the college admissions process is a numbers game. Is it? To an extent it is. Average grades and/or average test scores do not get your child into a top school. The good news is a student can excel in any college and use the time there as a springboard to a successful life.

If you are a parent who attended college, you probably took the SAT. Remember that test? The one where you sat for three hours on a Saturday morning with a number two pencil? Do you recall having to fill in the bubbles on the answer sheet? Did you hope that you did really well so you could get into the school of your choice? Do you remember liking it? Few of us liked it, but we realized that doing well on this test might help us to get into the college (or colleges!) of our dreams. Well, very little has changed in ten, twenty, thirty, or forty years—except that college admissions overall are more competitive, and this and other tests have taken over much of the admissions process. While standardized tests will never be the most important factor in determining college admissions—having good grades in challenging classes is essential—they are a big piece of the puzzle, and understanding which tests your child should take and when to do so can be confusing.

The SAT is still "the big test." Since 1926, when it began as a series of questions that were developed by the U.S. Army to select World War I military recruits, it has been the dominant admissions test for aspiring college students. It contains three sections (Critical Reading, Math, and Writing), with each scored out of 800 (for a total of 2400), and is offered seven times each year (October, November, December, January, March, May, and June). It has an accompanying practice test—the PSAT—offered to high school students across the country in the fall of junior year. Some schools even let sophomores take the PSAT as a pre-practice test, with the expectation that students will take the SAT at least once as a junior and again as a senior. Beginning March 2016, the class of 2017 is the first class to take the redesigned SAT.

Although many Midwestern and Southern US students take the ACT each year, the SAT I and SAT II Subject Tests seem to dominate the world of competitive college admissions. But an increasing number of colleges and universities across the country now accept the ACT as a suitable alternative to the SAT. Both tests have slightly different formats, and many schools do not have a preference between the two. Students should prepare for the test they feel most comfortable with, after taking a diagnostic test for both with a tutor, or by simply taking the PSAT or the PLAN. The PLAN is the practice ACT exam administered to sophomores at a school or district's discretion.

"Believe it or not, the college admissions process starts in the eighth grade."

When should my child start taking standardized tests?

The SAT I can be taken as early as the sixth or seventh grade. Research the possibility of taking the SAT I to qualify for advanced programs such as the Johns Hopkins Center for Talented Youth.

Most students who aspire to top colleges usually take their first SAT I in their freshman or sophomore year. Spring of junior year is too late. A reasonable plan for these students would be to take one in the spring of sophomore year and then note the score comparison with the PSAT, usually taken in October of junior year. SAT II Subject Tests (formerly known as Achievements) are one-hour exams offered at the conclusion of high school courses such as biology, French, Spanish and chemistry. Students can use these Subject Tests to demonstrate their capabilities in a certain course, and begin taking them as early as the ninth grade. Students should always consult their teachers or guidance counselors about the Subject Tests to see if their course material prepares them for these exams.

BEWARE: Some schools expect students to submit all of their scores, no matter how good or not so good they are. Students should only take tests that they are confident they will do well on and feel ready for. Other than that, the SAT or ACT need to be taken no later than June of junior year, with the expectation of taking it again as a senior.

The Case for Professional Test Prep

Your child's scores will play a part in their admission to college—possibly their financial aid to college—and their placement in certain courses; the higher the scores, the better. You may be surprised to learn how many applicants to America's top colleges have scores approaching perfection on the SAT I. An equally surprising number also have perfect 800s on their Subject Tests.

So, would it be beneficial for my child to take a test prep course? If you can afford it, then yes; you bite the bullet and get your child a tutor who will help them to get the best score possible. That is not to say that you need to spend hundreds or thousands of dollars. Rather, assess your price point and find a reputable tutor or tutoring company willing to work with you and your child. Sure, the College Board that administers the SAT has done a fantastic job in recent years collaborating with Khan Academy to offer free SAT prep, but the jury is still out on how well this preparation works and who it works for. I am a big advocate for hiring someone who knows how to take these tests and will show your kid the way. Is it gaming the test? No, it's preparing. It's utilizing your resources to give your kid an advantage in a process that is often unfair.

If a tutor or private test prep is not in your budget, then preparation of any kind helps. Use the free online preparation courses for students, or they can familiarize themselves with tests by using study books (many come with digital components that make practice very convenient) from a local bookstore or library; unfortunately, few students have the discipline to learn the strategies to excel on these tests on their own. Those who do are usually already at the top of their classes, or have been unusually strong test takers for a long time. If this is the case, minimal preparation is fine, but an applicant should never do these tests without having done some prior practice.

"As much as colleges like to know your child is well-rounded, the depth of their involvement matters more than spreading themselves too thin."

3. Extracurricular Resumes

Colleges care a great deal about students' activities outside of school hours. They are looking for curious and involved young people to populate their incoming class, and nothing will indicate this more than a track record of doing well in school AND having impact outside the classroom. So, your students should not hold back writing about extracurricular activities on the Common Application.

What counts as an extracurricular activity? Anything outside of class work—to which dedicated hours of work or involvement have been committed, and better yet, gotten results. This includes, but is not limited to, competing on sport and academic teams, taking care of chronically-ill relatives, traveling with a church or community choir, reading to children at a hospital, doing house chores for an elderly neighbor every weekend, making art for sale, or running some other small business.

The list should begin with activities to which a significant number of hours, months, and perhaps even years, have been dedicated. Why? As much as colleges like to know students are well-rounded, the depth of their involvement matters more than the spread. For example, it speaks better to dedication and leadership abilities if students can identify three or four activities in which they have participated, excelled, and taken on increasingly major roles for three years of high school, rather than ten activities done for a few months each.

Students should avoid listing one-off activities that lasted just a few hours, unless it is particularly impressive (like interviewing the local mayor or the President of the United States for the school newspaper). Of course, students should include those activities that have been meaningful to them—the ones that have impacted them so greatly they may have written about them in one of their college essays.

If your child is a very active student or a prodigy, with several years of involvement and a significant impact in more than ten activities to prove it, decide if all these activities need to be included on the list. A shortlist can be made that includes only the most impressive ones, combining similar ones (school newspaper reporter and school newspaper editor can be listed on one line instead of two), or save some for the Additional Information section.

Your students need to be smart in choosing and talking about these activities! An extracurricular resume can be used to show a student's passion in a certain area. For example, for students applying to schools that care about recruiting strong writers, they should list their most meaningful writing activities. For students hoping to get an athletic scholarship as well, they could showcase their most impressive sports achievements in addition to the writing ones—by doing so, they have transformed themselves from strong athletes into strong athletes who are strong writers (impressive and competitive). And for those who have done some unusual-but-legal activity, like training animals, for even a few months, prioritize listing it over less memorable activities done for similar time periods. It can become a memorable piece of information or a conversation piece. Who wouldn't want to interview the applicant who can talk to dolphins?

"Your child should make the kind of impression in high school that he or she wants to share with a college."

4. Recommendations

Your students should approach their teachers in the spring of their junior year about writing recommendations. They need to be wise and choose teachers who can attest to their academic prowess and strength of character, and ones who are aware of their college and life ambitions. Ideally, these teachers will come from disparate disciplines: English and math, or science and history, for example. Having two recommendations from similar courses like English and history, or science and math may carry repetitive detail and fail to show his or her versatility as a student. You want colleges to see your child as a versatile student who excels.

Remember that teachers are flooded with their regular work and write recommendations for students as an additional task. Make things easier for them, and improve the quality of the recommendations, by ensuring that your child's teacher is aware of his or her accomplishments and the reason your child wishes to attend college. If already compiled, have your child share his or her extracurricular resume and drafted college application essay with a teacher, if your child is comfortable doing so. Better yet, have your child ask for a few minutes of the teacher's time to talk about your child's extracurricular involvement and college ambitions, so the teacher can write something less generic and more personal.

Students have the power to "write their own recommendation." Impress this particularly upon your freshman and sophomore child. The way they use their time in school and outside of school, how they contribute to their classes, their intellectual curiosity, and the grades they earn, as well as how they relate to their peers are all fair game for a teacher recommendation. These are all things that students have the power to control and craft. They need to make the kind of impression in high school that they would want to convey to a college.

"A well-written college essay is a game changer... *Through reading your child's essays, admissions officers should begin to get excited at the thought of having your child on campus.*"

5. Essays

There are two things to remember about college application essays. College essays are important because they give students a chance to speak directly with the admissions committee. A well-written college essay is a game changer.

I always say that the essay portion is the hardest part of the college application process. Grades are a product of four years of hard work; standardized test scores, and even teacher recommendations, are a result of months—if not years—of preparation. Similarly, college application essays require months of strategic and persistent brainstorming, writing, and revising. Essays are, however, uniquely the element of the application that requires the most self-reflection and thought on the part of the student.

Students need to submit one-of-a-kind essays that show self-reflection, clarity, and depth because those are the most impactful kinds. By reading your child's essays, admissions officers should begin to salivate at the thought of having your child on their campus. Paint a picture through the Common Application and supplemental essays that your children are prepared to excel on and contribute to the college campus, are mature and know themselves well, and are excited about the chance to go to college —the student in the essay must be memorable.

Ideally, brainstorming begins in the spring of your child's junior year. Typically, the essay prompts will ask the student to reveal something about him or herself. Use the summer wisely. No one is at the beach seven days a week for three months. Taking two to three hours per week in the summertime to think up and draft one personal essay and two to three supplemental essays is a sensible use of your child's time.

After eight to twelve weeks of summer vacation, there is no excusable reason for your child not to have a personal essay and one to three additional essays drafted. Even an hour per week will be helpful because the chaos of the opening weeks of school as a senior can be overwhelming for many students. Classes, standardized tests, games, homecoming, and other social activities can all encroach on their time and lead to writer's paralysis. It is imperative for them to start this process before senior year.

Another great reason to use the summer before senior year as a time to start writing essays is that the student can get a leg up on asking English teachers and counselors for help. Recognize that teachers and school counselors have a love-hate relationship with the start of the school year. While they are usually eager to get back into the rhythm of their jobs, there are way too many meetings and other opening of school 'stuff' that bombard them for the first few weeks. Expecting them to be available early on is hard. If your student has a desire to complete college applications by late September or early October, it is best to work with teachers and counselors during the summer. They will be thankful to you for the consideration!

There is no formula to write an impactful college essay. However, memorable essays have certain characteristics. Primary among them is that the essay must—I repeat, MUST—grab the reader's attention from the first line. Even if students feel it's not their style or they hate to write, or think the body and conclusion matter most, they are fooling themselves. Students need to draw the reader in and then hold their attention by telling them something about themselves that they would never learn from somewhere else in the application.

THE TEN COMMANDMENTS OF WRITING A COLLEGE ESSAY

1. **Choose a topic you care about.** Some schools give you one topic, some schools have an open question, and some schools give you a choice of multiple topics. Make sure you answer the question for each school you are applying to—especially if you are using the same essay for more than one school.

   Write about something you care about that has meaning to you. There are no wrong topics—just wrong treatments of those topics. If you have been affected by an experience, you can write a more effective essay about it. Don't worry about what other students may be writing. Write in your own voice.

2. **Try to stick to experience.** It will reveal more about you than an essay about an abstract topic outside of your experience.

3. **Keep it simple.** Be clear and direct; don't bury your point. Make it easy to understand. Strive for economy, precision and clarity.

4. **Throw away the thesaurus.** Don't try to impress us by using big words when unnecessary. It's easy to spot a thesaurus essay. Again, you risk losing your own voice.

5. **Avoid generalities wherever possible.** Narrow your focus, and use details and anecdotes. This will make it more vivid for your readers. It will make it come alive. This is true even for essays that seem to demand general answers.

6. **Find a voice.** This is the most difficult part. Ideally, your essay should sound like your conversation at its best. Don't try to sound the way you think we want you to sound. Sometimes, it's difficult to find a voice but it is worthwhile. A clear voice will make us say, "I feel like I know this person," or "I'd really like to meet this person."

7. **Edit.** Spend some time on it. Write it, put it away, and rewrite it. Pare it down. Try to confine it to a reasonable space. Make your essay only as long as it needs to be.

8. **Don't over-edit.** Certainly revise it, but trust yourself. Many of the best essays convey a sense of spontaneity. As soon as you think the essay communicates a sense of who you are—submit it.

9. **Get someone to proofread.** Does it say what you want it to? Does it get your point across? Is the punctuation correct? Are there typos?

10. **But not too many proofreaders!** You will risk sounding like those other people think you should sound. Again, trust yourself.

Source: Oberlin College

And now that you know what your children should do, here are a few tips on what they should not do:

- **Do NOT rehash the resume in an essay**. Listing their activities and accomplishments in prose is a waste of an opportunity. Colleges will have seen these accomplishments somewhere else on the application, and reading about them is boring. Instead, have them tell WHY an activity or accomplishment is meaningful, or HOW a personal achievement was used to benefit others.

- **Do NOT use an essay to complain.** Your children should refrain from complaining about you, their peers, teachers, school, rules, and so on; teenage angst is a tired topic. No one wants to hear about how a student was treated badly as this will surely come off as angry or bitter. Help them paint a person with a positive outlook. Even if writing about a challenge, students should focus on how they overcame it, the lessons they learned, or how they were empowered by the experience to do well in the future. College is a place for creative problem solvers—not problem pushers. Think about it: would you hurry to admit students whose essays complain about having been bullied in high school and how they can't wait to 'start over' in college? Or, who you rather admit those who instead write about their love for creating harmonious campus communities by making anti-

72

bullying public art, which resulted from their experiences of being bullied? "Away with the whiner! Admit that anti-bullying artist." I can hear it now.

- **Do NOT lie.** Sounds simple enough, right? Lying is losing, and if your child is found out, there's almost a guarantee that the college will rescind their offer of admission. Being dishonest does not set a good tone for a burgeoning relationship with a place where your child's next four years may be spent.

Be sure to download a worksheet to help you and your child at strategicadmissionsadvice.com/bookstore

Chapter 5

HOW TO USE THE
HIGH SCHOOL YEARS

"Each year, each season (fall, winter, spring, and summer) of your child's high school career, something can be done to increase his or her chances of having college choices."

HOW TO USE THE HIGH SCHOOL YEARS

There are over three thousand colleges and universities in the United States, yet many of our clients only want to talk about fifty of them. In order to have the best choices, you and your child must have information about all possible choices and be open to them.

To enjoy the best choices in life, time must be used strategically, and time in high school must be used well. Each year, each season (fall, winter, spring, and summer) of your child's high school career, something can be done to maximize his or her chances of having college choices. I have broken the process down into four years.

"No year is more important than the junior year. The stakes are high and colleges are expecting students to tackle junior year with confidence and a sense of urgency."

Freshman Year

Your freshman child should step into the high school experience with curiosity and confidence, and with the understanding that it is important to build a strong academic foundation: freshman year grades count in the college admissions process because they can be used as evidence of having built a track record of excellence. High school GPA and class rank have begun to be tabulated. Your child must take the appropriate prerequisite courses now to be able to take AP and other challenging courses later—and consider taking AP classes if they are available. They should consider taking an SAT I in January to get some testing experience, and intern or volunteer in the summertime.

Some other ways for your child to use freshman year:

- **Your child needs to study hard** to get the best grades possible.
- **Your child should strengthen vocabulary** by reading.
- **Your student can explore various extracurricular activities and undertake volunteer work.** Starting as a freshman may lead to a leadership position as a junior or a senior.
- **Your son or daughter should meet his or her high school guidance counselor** and discuss academic plans for the next four years.
- **Does your child need to prepare to take an SAT II Subject Test in June?**
- **Do you have a child who is an athlete who needs to review the NCAA (National Collegiate Athletic Association) eligibility requirements?** There are certain courses required in high school to be a student-athlete in college.

Sophomore Year

Your students heading into sophomore year should pay attention to the courses and activities that bring them joy and those that do not. This is the time for them to develop an understanding of who they are and what courses appeal to them most. They must focus on maintaining a strong GPA, and schedule taking APs—if this is possible at their school. They should deepen or diversify their involvement in extracurricular activities, especially service activities.

They can take another SAT I exam in the spring. They should score higher than as a freshman. Have students begin reading books from college readings lists (available online), as now both writing skills and vocabulary should be growing. Be sure to plan a meaningful summer filled with work or volunteer activities.

Some other ways for students to use sophomore year:

- **In September, your students should ask their guidance counselors if they are a candidate to take the PSAT in October.**

- **Your students should prepare to take an SAT II Subject Test in June, if applicable.** Many sophomores take the SAT II test in chemistry or world history, depending on their high school's curriculum. Many colleges require or recommend one or more of the **SAT II Subject Tests** for admission or placement.

- **Your students should take stock of their summer schedule.** They should consider taking a summer course at a local college, in another state, or abroad. They may also consider working or volunteering.

- **During the summer, your students may consider signing up for a PSAT/SAT prep course**, and test using computer software or practice tests in books designed to familiarize them with standardized tests.

- **They can do a personality/college/career assessment.** It is helpful for your students to go into junior year with a plan.

Junior Year

No year is more important than junior year. This is when students have matured enough academically to take AP or advanced courses and do well. The stakes are high and colleges are expecting your students to tackle junior year with confidence and a sense of urgency. This is their year when grades, scores, and depth of activities matter. It is also the time for them to demonstrate interest in a college by visiting the campus, time for them to decide which teachers will write recommendations, and time to decide to which schools they will tentatively apply.

Students should go into junior year with a firm plan for when they are going to take standardized tests. By then, your child should have identified how to prepare—with or without a tutor.

This is the year when students should take the PSAT in the fall, the real SAT or ACT in the winter, and visit colleges throughout the year. Applying to college is less than a year away; those who win are those who are most prepared.

Your junior students need to pay close attention to this schedule to use this year strategically:

"The scholarship and financial aid processes have very strict deadlines and need careful attention in order for your students to meet them."

Fall

- **Your child registers for the October PSAT**. The Preliminary Standardized Assessment Test is a "practice" SAT that has some implications. The high school should have the necessary forms to register for it. This test usually triggers colleges to start emailing students and sending emails to market their school. It is also the test that determines National Merit Scholarship eligibility as well as National Achievement (African-American students) and National Hispanic Scholars. These scores do not have any impact on their actual college admission.

- **Your child's school guidance counselor should know your child's name**. If your child did not meet with the school counselor as a sophomore to review the junior schedule, now is the time to do it. You'll want them to confirm that your child is taking the right courses for junior and senior years—ones that should be able to help with the college admissions process.

- **Try to visit three to five schools with your child before March.** Many schools are closed for Columbus Day (October), Veterans Day (November), and Presidents' Day (February). Visit several college campuses with your child and ask your child: "Do you see yourself here?" "Can you thrive academically here?" These questions are critical to a student's self-exploration. These questions should not be asked for the first time as a first-semester senior.

Winter

- **It is time for them to hone in on academic and extracurricular interests** to have clarity about the kind of college that will help them keep developing these interests.

- **Review PSAT results with your child.** These scores should be received in December. Read the score report and consult a tutor, school counselor, or independent counselor to discuss ways for them to improve for future tests.

- **It is time for them to register for the January and/or March SAT and/or February and/or April ACT.**

- **Students should start to craft a list of ten to fifteen schools to possibly apply to**. They can use online tools to investigate further and discuss with their schools or independent counselors. Does your child's school use Naviance? This is a great tool to show how many students in recent years from a particular high school applied to certain universities. It can help gauge admissibility. Ultimately, the schools on the list should fit what the student wants out of college: academic program, size, location, cost, etc. Chances of admittance can be sensed based on the average achievements of the college's last incoming class.

Spring

- **Have you and your child visited three to five schools?** By now, you should have identified likes and dislikes about each one.

- **Discuss the realities of college costs with your child.** The scholarship and financial aid processes have very strict deadlines and need careful attention in order to meet them. Once you have your tax information from the previous year, assess what the Expected Family Contribution should be for college.

- **It is time for your child to register for the May/June SAT Reasoning Test and/or the May/June SAT Subject Tests and/or and June ACT Test.** Please note: not all SAT Subject Tests are given on every test date. Check the calendar carefully to determine when certain Subject Tests are offered. **They should also register for AP (Advanced Placement) exams, if applicable.**

- **Your students should confirm their senior schedule.** Are they taking enough advanced courses? Too many? Students are to speak with their school or independent counselor about their upcoming course loads and make sure that it is challenging and appropriate for them.

- **Encourage your students to research summer jobs or apply for special summer academic or enrichment programs.** Summer activities can be critical to showing how invested students are in a specific discipline. Working students can also save part of their earnings to cover the expense of moving to college or expenses while at school.

- **Go with your child to a college fair.** There are regional fairs that distribute lots of information about schools and scholarships. Meet admissions representatives from certain schools and begin to build a rapport. Many of these admissions officers will actually be the regional readers for your child's application, and may visit your child's school again in the fall.

- **Remind your students to ask two teachers to write recommendations.**

- **Encourage your student to set up summer interviews as early as possible—interview times become booked quickly!** Many schools offer interviews as part of their admissions process. Even if they are optional, doing an interviews is always a good idea because it shows interest, enthusiasm and initiative. Also, encourage your students to do a practice interview with their school or independent counselor. Remember, interviews are solely conversations, and are usually more informative that evaluative.

Summer

- **Consider enrolling your child in an application boot camp.** The ones offered by Strategic Admissions Advice help students to refine their college lists, start their essays and applications as well as set up manageable timelines to complete all of the necessary components.

- **You and your child can refine his or her college list to seven to twelve schools** that are potentially good matches.

- **Your students should start their essays!** Most schools will require a personal essay, and many will ask for supplemental essays. The more written over the summer, the less stressful the fall will be.

- **Your students may begin their applications!** The Common Application is available now and is accepted by over one thousand schools across the United States and abroad. It is strictly online and can be tedious. Students need to take their time, and enlist guidance from you or a counselor to ensure they complete it with accurate information that represents them well.

- **For your student-athletes who plan on playing in college, it is time to contact college coaches** and ask about intercollegiate and intramural sports programs and athletic scholarships. Complete the NCAA Initial-Eligibility

Clearinghouse form for students who hope to play Division I or II sports.

- **If your child is an artist,** collect writing samples or assemble portfolios or audition tapes.

- **For those families who haven't already, visit schools now.** Although it is ideal to visit colleges during the academic year, going in the summer will be valuable. Colleges usually start in August and everyone is refreshed from the summer. Your students should consider reaching out to professors in their chosen fields and meeting with them during the campus visit. The more information students have about a school, the better their essay might be, and the more interest they will show. Admission offices employ their students to give tours and answer questions from prospective students and their parents.

Senior Year

This is the big year. Hopefully, you and your child have prepared so well in sophomore and junior years that all of you can move comfortably into the home stretch.

If it will not affect the time your child is able to spend on college applications, or plunge his or her GPA, have your child consider taking a few more AP courses in the fall —preferably in areas that your child intends to pursue in college. Selective schools expect to see that students have taken between four and twelve AP courses over their high school careers, and have excelled in them; the focus should be on doing well in the courses, not simply taking a large number of them. Also, at this time they need to approach teachers to write recommendations, if not done in the summer. They will then follow up with recommendation writers and track the application progress with colleges. It is the student's responsibility to ensure that all pieces of the application are submitted on time. They need to keep meticulous tracking details on the progress of the various applications.

Some of your students may want to consider Early Decision or Early Action for clear, first-choice picks. It is time for them to register for the October SAT I, if needed. Depending on how the summer was used, it may be essay time. At this stage, your children and their school's college counselors should be speaking regularly. Your children should feel they are getting quality advice on the application and transitioning to college processes.

Early Decision/Action letters arrive in early-to-mid December. Regular decision letters arrive mid-March through mid-April. While waiting for them, you and your child should educate yourselves about negotiating financial aid offers. Your students should be working closely with college counselors to negotiate waitlist offers or say yes to acceptance offers. They will then follow through and enroll in the college of their choice.

Congratulations! Your strategic work has resulted in college admissions success for your child.

I know we've given you a lot of information in this chapter, but don't worry—we've created a calendar for you. Just visit: strategicadmissionsadvice.com/bookstore

Chapter 6

HOW PARENTS AND SCHOOL COUNSELORS CAN WORK COOPERATIVELY

"This is not the time for you to take a backseat in the college application process."

HOW PARENTS AND SCHOOL COUNSELORS CAN WORK COOPERATIVELY

Students' school counselors can play a large role in their college application preparation process. I want you and your child to know what they should expect from their guidance counselors, and what your child should be doing on their own to maximize their potential in this process. When your students seeks guidance from college counseling professionals, they want to feel safe and secure, knowing they are doing their best. The knowledge you have gained from this book should help you assess how well your child's counselor is carrying out their role.

"Too often, I see families that are naïve, and therefore negligent, with respect to the time, energy and strategy that goes into this process. On the other hand, some families are too uptight."

With all the help your child is receiving from both school and independent counselors, this is not the time for you to take a backseat in the college application process. As high schools grow, many public and private school guidance offices are dwindling in size. In both private and public schools, many people who have made this their lifelong career do not have the energy or ability to change with the times. I cannot begin to tell you how many school counselors have not embraced technology as an efficient way to execute the college admissions process. Too many counselors are formulaic in their approach to crafting school lists, and not critical enough to brainstorm strong essay topics. Very few school counselors help students revise essays and proofread applications. This is a problem. When school counselors are unable, for whatever reasons, to meet their students' needs and do their jobs, teenagers suffer.

I believe some families are not proactive enough in their preparation for the college application process. Too often, I see families who are naïve—and therefore negligent—with respect to the time, energy, and strategy that goes into this process. On the other hand, some families are too uptight—they are usually convinced that an outside counselor is lecherous and crooked, and their school counselor won't be thorough. I know *many* excellent school counselors and I honestly believe that most are experienced, conscientious educators. The extraordinary school counselors make a consistent effort to edify themselves by constantly learning about schools, programs, and so on, and do a superb job with their counseling.

However, in any industry, there are many overworked professionals who cannot dedicate the time and energy that a nervous student and family deserve. As an independent consultant, I will walk you through the demanding, but doable, process of securing a place in college. My years of admissions experience shaped the roadmap that I share with my families. This roadmap will take you through each action you should take—whether you begin your process in middle school or senior year. My road map to success will minimize stress and allow you to enjoy the last couple of years before your child goes off to college.

Glaringly Intentional Omission

As this book comes to a close—only the glossary is to follow—you may ask yourself why I only mentioned money and the college application process once. I get this question all the time: "Do you help kids to find scholarships?" "Do you help with financial aid?" The answer to both of those questions, right now, is "no."

I am an admissions expert, not a financial aid specialist. I have spent twenty years working with fairly affluent families who are not overly concerned with paying for college. I understand that this is a small part of the population, and that to reach more people, to help more people, there needs to be some kind of financial assistance when it comes to helping folks to understand how to pay for college.

I am working on it. As this book goes to print, I am confident that this time next year we will have a person on staff who will be a resource for more financial aid questions. It's important to me that we do not neglect students and families who need this advice.

GLOSSARY

Accreditation—The recognition by an outside agency that a school maintains high standards, which enables students to qualify for admission to other accredited institutions.

Admission Requirements—A set of rules established by each college for a student to be accepted.

Advanced Placement (AP)—A system by which college freshmen may bypass entry-level courses by proving that they have already taken the equivalent in high school. Credit may be awarded if a student earns a certain grade on an AP exam taken in high school.

Advanced Standing—Admission status when a student has completed more than 12 college credits.

Aid Package—A combination of aid (scholarships, grants, loans, and work study) determined by the college financial aid office.

American College Test (ACT)—A four-year college admissions test covering English, Math, Reading and Science.

Bachelor's Degree—The degree awarded for completing a college program of at least four years of academic work. Usually, this degree is either a Bachelor of Arts (B.A.) or a Bachelor of Science (B.S.).

College Board—A nonprofit organization that provides tests and many other educational services for students, schools and colleges.

College Catalog—A publication by a college describing services and courses offered, as well as requirements for admission and degrees. The college counselor at your high school may have a selection of college catalogs which include college addresses.

College Scholarship Service (CSS) PROFILE—A financial aid form used by many private colleges to award private, non-federal funds.

Common Core Curriculum—A national initiative that specifies what high school students should know at each grade level, and describes the skills that they must acquire in order to achieve college or career readiness.

Cumulative Record—The complete record of all courses and grades earned. A student transcript is a copy of his/her cumulative record.

Degree—A diploma given as official recognition for satisfactory completion of a course of study. A four-year degree is usually a B.A. (Bachelor of Arts) or B.S. (Bachelor of Science.) A five- or six-year degree is often a M.A. (Master of Arts) or M.S. (Master of Science.) A Doctoral degree (Ph.D.) requires five or more additional years beyond the B.A. or B.S.

Early Action—Highly qualified candidates who apply early may receive offers of college admission by mid-December. An Early Action plan does not allow an institution to request an applicant to make a prior commitment to matriculate, indicate college preferences, or make any response to an offer of admission until the traditional candidates reply date (usually in May).

Early Decision—Some colleges offer to notify applicants of acceptance or rejection during the first semester of their senior year. There are two types of early decision plans: the single choice plan—in which students cannot apply to another college until they have been notified by the early decision college; and, the first-choice plan—students may apply to other colleges, but name the early decision college as their first choice and agree to enroll at that college and withdraw all other applications if accepted. For further information, contact the college admissions office.

Economically Disadvantaged—Any individual or family whose annual earnings meet the United States Department of Labor definition of low income.

Elective—A course needed for graduation credit, but one that does not meet a specific course requirement.

Fee Waiver—A form available to students, whose eligibility is primarily determined by membership in a family with annual income falling within guidelines based on number of dependents and family income. The Fee Waiver is submitted instead of money when applying for college testing or admission.

Financial Aid—Scholarships, loans, grants, and/or a part-time job given to a student with financial need. The "financial aid package" of funds is determined by family financial need and the availability of college or government funds.

Financial Need—The difference between your expected contribution and the school's student budget; also known as financial aid eligibility.

Free Application for Federal Student Aid (FAFSA)—The federal application form required to apply for financial aid, including grants, loans, and work-study programs.

Full-time Student—Generally, a college student who takes a minimum of either 12 units per quarter or semester. This minimum number of units is usually required to maintain financial eligibility.

General Education Requirements—A specific group of courses from different academic areas required for any degree at some colleges. The general education requirements are described in each college catalog; also called Breadth Requirements.

Grade Point Average (GPA)—The average number of grade points earned divided by the number of credits attempted.

Grants—Financial aid that does not need to be repaid; usually awarded based on need, but can be awarded for academic achievement, special skill, talent, heritage or other criteria.

Impacted Program or Major—An overcrowded program or major in which there are many more applications than available spaces; supplementary admissions criteria often must be met for consideration.

Independent College—A school not supported by state taxes.

International Baccalaureate (IB) —A course of study that allows high school students to satisfy admission requirements of universities in more than 70 countries. Students can earn university credit for scores of 5 or higher on IB Higher Level examinations.

Liberal Arts College—A college in which the emphasis is on a program of philosophy, literature, history, languages, and basic science.

Lower Division—The courses usually taken during the first two years of a four-year college program. The classes are usually introductory or general education requirements.

Major—A student's main field of study in college.

Master's Degree—The degree given for completing a one- to two-year course of study beyond a Bachelor's Degree. Some Masters Degrees are Master of Arts (M.A.), Master of Science (M.S.), Master of Business Administration (M.B.A.), and Master of Fine Arts (M.F.A.).

Minor—A subject-area emphasis earned by completing approximately 18 credits in an area outside a student's major department.

Part-time Student—A college student who takes less than a full-time (12 units) schedule of classes and is ineligible for many financial aid programs.

Pell Grant—Financial aid from the federal government available to students with significant financial need, to be used at many types of colleges and vocational schools.

Preliminary Scholastic Aptitude Test/National Merit Scholarship Qualifying Test (PSAT/NMSQT)—A shortened version of the SAT offered in October to high school juniors and below. The scores are helpful in college admission planning and/or qualifying for National Merit Scholarships.

Prerequisites—Courses, test scores, and/or grade-level classes that must be completed before taking a specific course.

Private College (Independent College)—A school which is not supported by state taxes.

Profile—Supplementary College Board financial aid document required by some private universities.

Qualified Acceptance—Occasionally, an institution postpones action on an application and will suggest that the applicant pursue a particular course in its summer session. Upon satisfactory completion of this course, the college agrees to accept the student for its regular degree programs at the beginning of the first or second semester.

Rolling Admissions—This means that a college gives an admissions decision as soon as possible after an application is completed, and does not specify a notification deadline. Usually, it is wise to apply early to such colleges since applications are usually not accepted once the admissions quota has been reached.

Reserve Officer's Training Corps (ROTC)—Many colleges have units of the Reserve Officer's Training Corps that offer two- and four-year programs of military training, culminating in an officer's commission. In some colleges, credit for the courses can be applied toward a degree. ROTC scholarships are available—which pay for full college costs.

SAT Test—A college admission exam measuring critical reading and math reasoning skills; also includes a writing section with multiple-choice questions and an essay.

SAT Subject Tests (Formerly called the SAT II)—One-hour exams offered in twenty different subjects. Required by some schools and/or some majors. Check each school's requirements carefully. Up to three SAT subject tests may be taken in one sitting.

Scholarship—A gift of money (which does not need to be repaid) given to recognize student achievement, skills, and talent. It may be based partly on financial need.

Statement of Intent to Register (SIR)—This form that must be returned to the college of the student's choice by a specified date (usually the beginning of May). It confirms the student's intent to register at the college and reserves a spot.

Student Aid Report (SAR)—A form distributed by the College Scholarship Service for the purpose of estimating the family contribution to a student's college costs.

Test of English as a Foreign Language (TOEFL)—An English language exam for foreign students used for admission purposes and for placement in college English classes.

Transcript—An official copy of high school or college grades earned by a student.

Transfer Courses—College courses which may be transferred to another college.

Transfer Major—Students who intend to transfer to a four-year college pursue a transfer major at a community college. This consists of the lower-division requirements for a major at a particular college.

Transfer Students—College students who transfer from one college to another, usually at the end of the sophomore year. Changing colleges during the junior or senior year, when the student is completing major requirements, is not recommended.

Tuition—The fee for instruction at a college or vocational school.

Unit—A fixed amount of scholastic study used as a basis for calculating academic credits. College units for a course often equal the number of hours per week that the course meets. You must earn a specific number of units to receive a degree.

Undergraduate—A college student who has not yet received a bachelor's degree.

Upper Division—The courses usually taken during the last two years of a four-year college program. The courses typically are advanced courses in one's major and other areas.

Wait List—In addition to accepting and rejecting applicants, many colleges place students on a wait list for admission. As accepted applicants decide to attend other colleges, the school will offer their places to students on the wait list.

Weighted Courses—A policy which rewards accelerated and/or advanced performance by giving a "bonus" grade point for designated courses.

Work Study—A federally funded program that makes part-time jobs available to students with financial need.

Reprinted with permission.

Contact us if you would like to take this journey together.

Call Us: (917) 727-1055

Email Us: inquiry@strategicadmissionsadvice.com

www.strategicadmissionsadvice.com

Follow Us on Social Media:

Twitter.com/ShereemHB

Facebook.com/strategicadmissionsadvice

Instagram.com/ShereemHB